CHANGING ZIP CODES

Finding Community Wherever You're Transplanted

CAROL G. STRATTON

CHANGING ZIP CODES: FINDING COMMUNITY WHEREVER
YOU'RE TRANSPLANTED
BY CAROL G. STRATTON
Published by Lighthouse Publishing of the Carolinas
2333 Barton Oaks Dr., Raleigh, NC, 27614

All scripture quotations, unless otherwise indicated, are taken from the
HOLY BIBLE, NEW INTERNATIONAL VERSION®. NIV®. Copyright ©
1973, 1978, 1984 by International Bible Society.
Used by permission of Zondervan. All rights reserved.

ISBN 978-0-9847655-5-3
Copyright © 2012 by Carol G. Stratton
Cover design by Jeffrey Holmes www.loosepaintart.com
Book design by Anna O'Brien www.behindthegift.com

Available in print from your local bookstore, online, or from the publisher
at: www.lighthousepublishingofthecarolinas.com

For more info on this book visit:
www.facebook.com/ChangingZipCodes
https://twitter.com/#!/carolgstratton
www.ChangingZipCodes.com

Library of Congress Cataloging-in-Publication Data
Stratton, Carol G., Changing Zip Codes: Finding Community Wherever
You're Transplanted / Carol Stratton.— 1st ed.

Printed in the United States of America

Table of Contents

Preparing for the Move

Shifting to a New Community

Introduction

"You both scored high on adventure," said our counselor as he checked our premarital personality tests. Three decades later I see how true those test scores were. Marrying a successful, entrepreneurial businessman plucked me out of my home state of California as we transplanted ourselves in Indiana, Ohio, Michigan, Illinois, South Carolina, and North Carolina. I feel blessed because I've been able to experience different kinds of climates, new friends, and cultures in our wonderful country.

The best result of these moves has been a closer connection to God. Far from becoming "flakey" by all the moving, I've become grounded as He's made me a more solid person in my walk of faith. My life has been enriched in countless ways. I've been stretched in many areas while learning He is my community—*first and foremost.*

As a frequent mover, I've had to learn to fit in quickly or sink. Every time I'd leave one community, I'd work hard to find another community in my new location. Sometimes it only took three months for me and my family to feel at home. In other areas I still felt like a stranger in the neighborhood after three years, but after twenty-two moves, I've learned that community starts with one's heart. Each time I'd step over the threshold of a new home, I'd pray for God to show me where I could find community. He has been faithful and, as a result, I have friends all over the country.

I've written this small book to encourage anyone who's had to pack and unpack their entire home, especially numerous times. Moving is like a giant spatula that scoops up your life and flips it over, leaving you to sort out kitchen utensils, children's toys, books, photos, appliances, old tax receipts, and lawnmowers in its wake. You may think you'll never be organized again and you'll never have a support group. I want to assure you that you will develop roots if you keep a good attitude and rely on your Heavenly Father for moral support.

Author Bio

Carol Stratton has written for several publications, including *InTouch* magazine and *Kyria*. She is a contributing writer for *Forsyth Woman* magazine and has been published in two anthologies, *Writing so Heaven Will be Different* and *Extraordinary Answers to Prayers*. She speaks to women's groups such as MOPS (Mothers of Preschoolers), and at national writers' conferences. She attended Capernwray Bible School in New Zealand. Carol and her husband live in North Carolina and have four children and two grandchildren. Her website, www. ChangingZipCodes.com, helps families who are relocating.

Endorsements

"Carol Stratton has chosen to write to a topic that is addressed in few other places: clinging to faith during times of change. The fresh daily format and encouraging, biblical insights will encourage anyone who is struggling through the idea of moving to a new location, as well as uplifting those who are joyfully anticipating a move."— **Darla Knoth**, Leadership Development/ Content Coordinator, National Women's Department, Assemblies of God

"After twenty-two moves, Carol Stratton is a relocation expert with a heart for the newcomer. Carol's warm and witty stories, based on personal experiences, offer hope and encouragement to anyone faced with a move." — **Florence Littauer**, International Author and Speaker, Founder of CLASSeminars ministry

"Having moved fourteen times, I find Carol's devotional book both encouraging and inspiring for anyone relocating. Filled with biblical principles, it keeps the reader focused on Christ during the upheaval of change that comes with moving. Her hands-on experience with relocating adds humor and warmth that will capture the heart of anyone who goes through the transition and adjustment of a move." — **Susan Miller**, Founder and President of Just Moved Ministry and author of *After the Boxes are Unpacked*

"Using wit, humor, and entertaining facts (even about Zip Codes), Carol Stratton provides helpful tips, insight, and cheerleading for those who are facing the "big move." She proves that God is everywhere, even among new neighbors, new coworkers, and new church members. Let her words encourage you."— **Dr. Dennis E. Hensley**, author *The Power of Positive Productivity*

"Knowing Carol, I realize her faith in God helped her trust me to help with their move. Carol has experienced many moves and knows the ins and outs. Enjoy her tips, words, and insights." — **Mary Jane O'Brien**, Top Realtor for F.C. Tucker Company, Inc.

"Carol Stratton lives what she teaches us in *Changing Zip Codes*. I have watched her life with admiration for many years. Her devotional is helpful for anyone in any situation any day of the week. I look forward to each page as Carol makes moving almost fun. She challenges us in so many practical ways and shows us how to serve God and find community where we're transplanted." — **Muriel Cook**, retired missionary, international speaker, counselor and author of *Kitchen Table Counseling*

"*Changing Zip Codes: Finding Community Wherever You're Transplanted* is for movers or anyone struggling with major life transitions. While using scripture and real stories from her twenty-two moves, author Carol Stratton motivates readers with encouragement, humor, and practical wisdom, reminding them that God is always at the other end of the moving van's trip. This upbeat 40-day devotional would make an excellent gift for anyone relocating." — **Michelle Medlock Adams**, award-winning author of more than 50 books and inspirational speaker (www.michellemedlockadams.com)

"Carol Stratton has written not only a meaningful and valuable devotional for those who are moving to a new location, but I see it also being very valuable for those moving into new life stages such as: the youngest child going off to school, empty nest, divorce, retirement, etc. *Changing Zip Codes* will be the perfect gift to bless many women, from the young to the young at heart, at any age in any stage of life." — **Mitzi Beach** ASID CAPS, www. LifesizingLady.com, "*Designing life for the second half*"

Being a Real Estate agent I deal with people every day who are totally stressed out and upset with the situation they find themselves in, that of losing control. So many pieces need to come together with changing homes, towns, states, schools, neighborhoods, etc. It is so helpful to have a resource to offer clients with devotionals, insight and prayers for one of the most stressful times in people's lives. Thanks for this invaluable tool. — **Margie Brady**, Broker/ Realtor Allen Tate Realty

Acknowledgements

We kid ourselves when we think we can write in a vacuum. I'm very thankful to those who have read my work and have contributed to my website, ChangingZipCodes.com. I have one perspective of community and I need the viewpoint of others, so I'm thankful to Cheri Cowell, Ann Hutchens, Laurie Long, Mollie Bond, Laura Warren, Irene Nielsen, Tammy Price, and Linda Schwert.

Thanks also to the many fine writers I've met at Write to Publish and CLASSeminars Writers Conference. A strong critique of a writer's work helps us with our craft while developing the proverbial "rhino skin."

Thanks for my 9-1-1 friends, Marge DeYoung and Chris Bos. They are great prayer partners. I also appreciate the time and effort of my Beta readers, Erica Key, Cynthia Key, Angie Hammond, Marnie Reber and Frankie Tipton for the extra set of eyes. Kudos to Seth Stratton, Gloria Graham, and Andrea Merrel for their meticulous editing, and my editor, Eddie Jones for his patience and helpfulness.

Thanks also to Susan Cox who listened patiently as I shared some of my stories. Now, there's one person who might have even more stories than me.

Thanks to my family, especially my husband John, who has always encouraged me to continue this long road of writing, and my children who have had to graciously change zip codes many times in their lives.

Helpful Websites

www.bestplaces.net

www.realtor.com

www.just-moved.org

www.uhaul.com

www.careerbuilders.com

www.wikihow.com

www.usps.com

www.MOPS.org

www.meetup.com

www.moms.meetup.com

www.city-data.com

www.greatschools.org/find-schools/

www.changingzipcodes.com

Zip Code Trivia

The word "zip" in zip codes stands for zoning improvement plan. The system started being used July 1, 1963.

- 12345 is Schenectady, NY.

- The highest number a code begins with is 9 and is West Coast.

- The lowest number is 0 and is the East Coast (and Alaska).

- Ketchikan, Alaska has the highest zip code: 99950.

- The least populated zip code is Loving County, TX.

- The White House's zip code is 20500 but there is a zip code plus a four digit number for the President and the First Lady.

- In 1964, Smokey Bear was so popular he was given his own zip code: 20252.

- Barefoot Bay in Brevard County, Florida is a mobile home park so large it has its own zip code: 32976.

- A mall in Glendale, California has its own zip code.

- A zip code in Centralia, Pennsylvania has been revoked by USPS because of an underground fire.

- The most densely populated zip code is 10162, the Upper East Side of Manhattan, in New York City.

Preparing for the Move

Day 1

Chains that don't chafe...

Now I want you to know, brothers, that what has happened to me has really served to advance the gospel. As a result, it has become clear throughout the whole palace guard and to everyone else that I am in chains for Christ. Because of my chains, most of the brothers in the Lord have been encouraged to speak the word of God more courageously and fearlessly.

Philippians 1:12-14 NIV

Chains are chains for one reason—they keep one object tied to another. We understand their usefulness with inanimate objects whether it means securing bicycles to a hitching post or keeping a gate locked at night. But when we feel bound to our circumstances, imaginary chains become a point of frustration. Perhaps one spouse is tied to selling a house while the other has to move ahead to start a new job or a married couple has been called to the mission field and they need to sell their house to help fund their ministry. Maybe we feel imprisoned in an area we don't like, but because of situations with family, and jobs, we are not free to leave.

When writing how his imprisonment had given him opportunities to share his faith, the Apostle Paul refused to fight his chains. History tells us that every four hours Paul was chained to a new prison guard and many became believers. The

Bible tells us that as a result of what happened to Paul, the gospel was advanced.

Seeing our life chains as a way to anchor us to God, helps us stop chaffing against them. Those miserable, weighty, iron links that seem to hold us down might be necessary to make us stop and do something we might not have done otherwise. When we are stuck in one place with few options, God often does His finest work. Being pinned to one place gives us time to think about our lives, to pray more, to communicate with others in our current community, and spend quality time worshipping our Lord.

God might even have a special project for us that we wouldn't have seen while flitting around in our previous life. A few years ago my husband and I found ourselves unemployed while trying to sell our house. Fourteen months of showing a house in a down market seemed like an eternity when we wanted to move on, but I have a 70,000 word novel to show for my time of house arrest.

Are you bound to your present circumstances? God may have you anchored for a reason. Look around you. Is there someone God wants you to befriend in order to share your faith? Release from anxiety often comes when we respond to our current situation while looking for opportunities to make good out of it.

When we quit fighting our chains, we may find a greater purpose in wearing them.

Day 2

Think it through…

Suppose one of you wants to build a tower. Will he not first sit down and estimate the cost to see if he has enough money to complete it?

Luke 14:28 NIV

Living in South Lake Tahoe, California seemed like a dream location for a new job. My husband and I had the Sierra Nevada Mountains in our backyard and one of the most beautiful lakes in the world only a few miles down the road. When my husband accepted a position managing a camp, I knew we'd hit pay dirt. I pictured us taking leisurely days off to hike the trails, boat the turquoise lake, and explore abandoned gold mine towns. In winter we'd ski down the powdery slopes.

Reality quickly slammed us. My husband worked almost seven days a week, on call like a country doctor. He faced strong-willed staff members, a flu epidemic that almost shut the camp down, an overturned boat (with the threat of the boater going into hypothermia), and a health department inspection… all within the first four months. My rose-colored view of his job turned gray from stress and led to exhaustion for both of us. Suddenly those snow-capped mountains didn't matter much. I missed seeing my husband as I craved an opportunity for him to have a day off.

Sometimes our dreams collide with practical life. We were newlyweds when we took the camp job. Our Tahoe experience taught us that we, as a couple, need to really think things through before we pull up stakes and jump into a new career. Though we both tend to come out high on the "craving adventure and change scale," we've learned through hard experiences to take time to research and understand the impact a move will make on our family. Planning and analyzing is essential. Seriously scrutinizing a possible move may save you dollars and heartache down the road.

Are you considering a move state to state or even just a change of houses in your town? God's word reminds us to count the cost. How will this possible relocation affect the emotional, financial, educational, and social needs of your family?

God wants the best for us and we can't always see the best without His guidance.

Day 3

Courage for the little things...

For I am the Lord, your God, who takes hold of your right hand and says to you, Do not fear; I will help you.

Isaiah 41:13 NIV

Sometimes I feel like I have courage for the larger things in life, like surviving a car accident, giving birth to a premature son, or spending time living in a foreign country. It's the little things where I fail, like fearing the walk into an unfamiliar church, unpacking and organizing a sea of boxes in my family room, or getting oriented to a new town. Yes, I can fly across the globe to a Bible college in New Zealand, but, "Please God, don't put me on a freeway two miles away from my new house!"

Our Heavenly Father offers courage for *all* situations. He doesn't rate our need and say, "You're on your own for this situation; it's only a 2.4 on the fear scale and I don't mess with such trivial situations." What kind of God would that make Him? No, He loves us enough to subdue our daily fears. When we do our part and take a first step, He will watch our back and take away our fear, but we need to make the first move.

In his book, *The Neurotic's Notebook,* Mignon McLaughlin says, "Courage can't see around the corner but goes anyway."

Lewis's outlook on courage is: "Courage is not simply one of the virtues, but the form of every virtue at the testing point."

If we are to be lean, strong men and women of faith, we can expect God to take us on some adventures where we know not where we are going. Courage opens the door and says "boo" to our fears.

What is your biggest fear about moving to a new area? Are you afraid your children won't make friends? You won't find a job? You will hate the weather? You'll never see your extended family? You will never grow to love that dark galley kitchen? Look your fears straight in the eye and take one little action today to conquer them. God is great at matching our timid first steps and will be there to keep us moving forward.

Sometimes all we have is a community of two, but sometimes that's enough…for a start.

Day 4

The partnership that dissolves...

...God is faithful, and he will not let you be tempted beyond your strength, but with the temptation will also provide the way of escape, that you may be able to endure it.

I Corinthians 10:13 RSV

Recently, the Bloomberg Report online stated the amount of homeowners filing for foreclosure will soon reach 5 percent. Banks, according to RealtyTrac, seized over a million homes in 2010.

Let's put this into perspective. If there were twenty families on your block, the odds are that one of them could be underwater in their mortgage and would soon have to forfeit the biggest investment in their lives. Every planted bush, painted wall, and backyard sandbox could be snatched from them as their personal finances descend into the largest financial sinkhole in history. Families could find themselves living in a different neighborhood or town because they had to downsize into apartments and other more modest housing. I've seen several couples end up in divorce court over an overwhelming mortgage.

So where is God?

God should be in our attitude. The Bible says He inhabits the praises of His people. He doesn't promise a roomy, four-bedroom home or a nice nest egg for retirement. He doesn't guarantee hassle-free child raising or stress-free jobs. He may bless us with material items or extremely well-behaved children, but nothing is for certain.

This promise, however, *is* for certain: He won't allow us to be tempted beyond our strength. He will provide a way to endure a trial. This reminds me of the old pressure cooker my mother used when she canned beans and tomatoes. Her large sealed pot allowed her to cook food quickly under ten-fifteen pounds of pressure. The top of the pot had a gauge to show how much pressure was in the pot. I remember watching the arrow on the gauge swing higher and higher as it ticked closer and closer to the "danger" end of the gauge. When that red needle moved all the way over to the right, I scurried out of the kitchen. I was sure the bomb was about to drop and we'd see glass and tomatoes splattered all over the kitchen. What I didn't realize was how my mother could regulate the pot's gauge and let out steam at any moment.

Just as my mother controlled the steam output of the pressure cooker, so God gives us grace to endure. He knows how much built-up steam we can handle and in His kindness, He unscrews the valve and lets the pressure out.

Today as you may be pulling up stakes to financially hunker down elsewhere, remember there is an escape. It may not be the escape you had planned for your family but we don't really know what plans are always the best for us. Foreclosure, as tragic as it is, isn't the end of the world.

Let's ask God today to release us from whatever financial stress and shame we might be experiencing in a weak economy.

Day 5

The divine magnet...

Commit to the Lord whatever you do, and your plans will succeed. The Lord works out everything for His own ends...

Proverbs 16:3-4 NIV

A five-hour commute gets old, but my husband did it every weekend for several months, burning a path to Cleveland, Ohio from West Michigan to see the family. We'd put our house up on the real estate market in the Buckeye state as my husband took a new job. Finally, after several months of no offers, I packed up the house, put the kids in the car, and drove to meet my husband in West Michigan. We were glad to be reunited but the stress of two mortgages grew burdensome. Every night around the dinner table, our family would pray for the Cleveland house to sell. We knew we were up against serious economic factors as Cleveland slipped into a recession. Weeks went by with no offers.

One night we received a call from our realtor. Trying not to chuckle, he shared what had happened. "I showed your house to a client today. He is an elderly gentleman who wouldn't seem to need a two-story home with four bedrooms in a neighborhood of young couples, but he insisted, so I took him to look at it. The client had just purchased a new Cadillac and wanted to test the garage to see if the car would fit. Unfortunately, he hit the side of the garage and damaged it."

"But," our realtor stopped for a dramatic pause, "Fortunately for you, he felt so bad about banging up the garage that he's made us an offer."

Loud cheers went up at our house.

Out of nowhere came a buyer. And that day, our family's faith increased dramatically.

Are you struggling with selling a house? He who has created the heavens and the earth has no problem drawing a buyer to your home. Even in a down market, there is always someone with money and a need for a house. I've seen it happen over and over. If there's still a "For Sale" sign in the yard, ask God to bring a buyer. He's the great magnet. The interested client may not be the one you had in mind, but a buyer is a buyer. Commit the sale of your home to God and He will become the best real estate agent you've ever had.

Day 6

All dressed down with somewhere to go...

Rejoice in the Lord always. I will say it again: Rejoice! Let your gentleness be evident to all. The Lord is near. Do not be anxious about anything, but in everything, by prayer and petition, with thanksgiving, present your requests to God.

Philippians 4:4-6 NIV

Out in front of his Bible school, David Weaver perched himself on top of a suitcase that held most of his worldly possessions. Even though he was sure he wanted to be a missionary, he didn't have next semester's tuition. Consequently, he found himself moving out of the dorm room and onto the school's front lawn.

If it had been me, I would have been kicking the side of my suitcase, calling home to cry on my mother's shoulder, or writing a very self-righteous letter to the president of the school. Not David. A man of strong faith, he sported a large smile and a positive attitude. He had tried every other means to raise funds and nothing had worked. So he just sat outside with a grin, knowing God would come through with a miracle.

Maybe you need a housing miracle. It might be selling a home and finding temporary shelter before you can move on. It might be an affordable mortgage. But whatever it is, know that

God is paying attention. Even though heaven seems mute, He has not forgotten your need. But our part is spelled out clearly in Philippians: we are to rejoice, rejoice again, and rejoice always. After we do that we are to present our requests to God in a thankful manner.

So let's review. Rejoice, rejoice again, and pray with thanksgiving—end of discussion. But when we are talking about a major relocation in our lives, it's a very difficult thing to do. That's when we bring God our "sacrifice of praise." It's a sacrifice because we have to give up our normal way of handling things—whining, worrying, and stressing. But to use David as an example, getting our attitude right opens the door for God to work. Want to hear the rest of the story?

As David perched outside the administration building, a lady from the office ran out to tell him they'd found him a place to stay. Two bachelors had a room in their house and David could room there for free. In addition, the house was right behind the school, within walking distance.

As he hauled his gear into his new home, the phone rang. One of the owners picked it up and with a puzzled look, motioned to his new roommate, "It's for you."

Someone from the school's office had called to tell him there was a job available and he'd better get over there, pronto. David explained how he was in a grubby T-shirt and jeans, but the caller insisted he needed to get there immediately.

He rushed over to the employment office. Standing in line with other applicants, he felt foolish in his grungy work clothes among the suits and ties of the other young men. Suddenly he saw one of the interviewers pointing at him. "Hey you, come up here right now."

Shocked, he walked to the front of the line.

"I need someone in construction and see you are dressed for work. Can you start right away?"

David shook his head in amazement. In one day he'd gone from being homeless to landing a good roof over his head and a job. What an awesome God.

Today as we feel overwhelmed with a move, let's remember God does pay attention. Our part is to keep a faithful attitude. You might try pulling out a suitcase and putting it by the front door as a reminder that God does provide.

Day 7

Keeping a loose grip...

. . . watch out! Be on your guard against all kinds of greed; a man's life does not consist in the abundance of his possessions.

Luke 12:15 NIV

"Do we have to leave my toys in this house?" asked my three-year-old daughter as she tugged on my sleeve. She couldn't comprehend life without her precious baby doll and Fisher Price hot pink Big Wheels car. I assured her she'd see her toys at the new house; they were just going to travel a long distance and we needed to keep them safe in boxes.

Children get attached to their toys and the loss of a favorite "blankie" or stuffed animal can be tragic. Fortunately, we outgrow our need for playthings. But every time I move, I have to release my hold on my surroundings. I like to do a last minute walk-through of an empty home I'm leaving. As I've ambled through, surveying the rooms, I have stopped at a favorite reading nook, stared at an attic with a skylight, and taken a second look at a screened porch where we've entertained guests. In one yard I said farewell to a perennial garden lovingly planted by previous owners with the blue delphinium and coral bells I'd anxiously waited for in spring. I've even mourned the ugly textured stucco on the walls of one living room where dust loved to make its home. Hardest, was walking past one particular laundry room where we'd penciled in the heights of our four children. I had visions of chopping out a section of the wall and taking it with me. What's a little hole, anyway?

When we pack up and move on, I've learned not to look back and covet a former home. It's just a structure sitting on a piece of land. We leave, knowing we will make the next house a refuge full of new memories. Pictures will hang above the same sofa, our china cabinet will be brimming with the same crockery, and our bookshelves will hold the same well-read favorites. I know I will find joy in my new surroundings.

Take time to grieve your old home. If you lived there any amount of time, you will have memories you'll treasure. Then after you mourn, look ahead for the gift of new memories.

They're coming.

Day 8

Sure miss that kosher deli...

The Israelites said to them, "If only we had died by the LORD's hand in Egypt! There we sat around pots of meat and ate all the food we wanted, but you have brought us out into this desert to starve this entire assembly to death."

Exodus 16:3 NIV

I sat on our bare family room floor surveying the boxes I had to unpack. I didn't want to move back into this house. My heart was back in another state where I liked our church and had made several friends quickly. Tears poured down my cheeks as I felt betrayed by God. It's like He gave me two bites of chocolate lava cake and then whisked it away from me. My tears turned into a tantrum. I liked the other town better and I just plain didn't want to move again. The other town had better restaurants, a better church, and the neighbors were friendly.

My husband had expanded our company and we relocated to another state. Things were humming along until September 11 happened. Like many Americans, we lost a lot of business; in fact our business was cut in half after that horrible national tragedy. We did a boomerang move, packing up and moving back up north to the house we weren't able to sell before we left.

Embarrassing? Yes. Necessary? Yes.

The ancient Egyptians had a history of abusing the Israelites.

They used the Israelites as a slave race to construct bricks under the scorching Egyptian sun. When the Hebrew workers wouldn't produce their daily quota of bricks, the Egyptian overseers would beat them. Moses observed the treatment of his fellow Hebrews and sought revenge by killing an Egyptian foreman. So when God provided countless plagues to allow the Hebrews to leave Egypt, you might think they would rejoice at their freedom. Instead they reminisced about the food, wishing God had just smote them back in the old country where they were a race of slaves.

Whining is not new. People have been whining at God for centuries. We need to keep good attitudes when we move to an area we don't particularly like. When I quit my crybaby attitude, God opened up new opportunities for friends and a new start-up church close by. He was just waiting for me to quit my bellyaching. Only God can see around the corner and He does what is best for you and me.

Today, let's give up our right to complain, giving God our annoyances and unfulfilled desires as a sacrificial offering.

Day 9

Why move?

There is a time for everything, and a season for every activity under heaven: a time to be born and a time to die, a time to plant and a time to uproot.

Ecclesiastes 3:1-2 NIV

One of my fellow bloggers, Mollie Bond, writes, "Seasons and scenery are the top two reasons I move. I may be moving because I need a change of scenery, but mostly I think it is because I need a change of seasons."

Other than a job or being near family, what are your reasons for moving? Is God calling you to a different city or are you just restless for change? There's no good or bad reason for moving per se, but we need to check our reasons for a move as some of us just have a little more gypsy blood than others.

New scenery always gives me a lift. I love to explore new stores, restaurants, and the local parks and historical sites. But I must always ask myself: "Is it time to move?" God's timetable is perfect and if we get ahead of Him, we're sure to have an unnecessary struggle.

I learned that lesson early. My dream place to settle down was the Sierra Nevada Mountains in California. I'd be hard-pressed to find a more pristine, emerald-colored lake as Lake

Tahoe, set in the most majestic peaks of the West. When my husband took the camp manager job with his college alma mater, it seemed too good to be true. It was.

With the many long hours, along with demanding staff and attendees, I rarely saw my new husband. As I drove from our house to the camp to "visit" him at dinner, I often fought waves of loneliness along with pangs of morning sickness. South Lake Tahoe is a very transient community with a third of the population turning over each year as casinos and skiing make up the town's economy. Making friends in the town was difficult. I learned that no matter how breathtaking the area, if I didn't have friends our view of the snow-capped mountains and ponderosa pines that lined our backyard mattered little. After a while, both of us wondered why we took the job.

What I learned from that move is to treasure community. Beauty, even with the most jaw-dropping views, can become as dull as last year's vacation postcard if I don't have friends. I'd rather be part of a good community even if I find it in the dumpiest town or the most backwater location. Scenery can lose its luster, but having community with solid friends can only grow brighter.

As you consider a move, ask yourself, "Why?" Are you in love with a dream that might not be realistic for your family's health? Do you hunger after excitement because you're just getting stale or restless in your hometown? Often God will stir us to move, but we need to be careful to be content if His real plan is to have us work on community right where we are. Moving or staying, pray that God will place you in the best community for you and your family.

Day 10

Left behind forever...

The two men (angels) said to Lot, "Do you have anyone else here sons-in-law, sons or daughters, or anyone else in the city that belongs to you: get them out of here, because we are going to destroy this place. The outcry to the Lord against its people is so great that he has sent us to destroy it." So Lot went out and spoke to his sons-in-laws. He said, "Hurry and get out of this place, because the Lord is about to destroy the city!" But his sons-in-law thought he was joking.

Genesis 19:12-14 NIV

Harry R. Truman, owner and caretaker of Mount St. Helens Lodge, lived with his sixteen cats on the mountain for fifty years. He neither knew nor wanted any other life. So, when officials commanded him to vacate the premises, he dug in his heels. At eighty-three years of age, no one was going to tell him what to do.

He believed the lodge was protected from a potential eruption because it was one mile away from the volcano. He also knew of a tremendous forest of trees that stood as a barricade between him and the volcano rim. Unfortunately, his belief was wrong. On May 18, 1980, the north side of the mountain erupted and covered his beloved lodge with 150 feet of ash and debris.

Sometimes we have more to gain from moving than staying

put. Harry, who loved his little piece of heaven, refused to believe the danger. Lot's sons-in-law had the same mind-set. They laughed at him thinking he was kidding when Lot insisted they move. They refused to heed the danger. Angels finally grabbed the hands of Lot, his wife, and his two daughters. The young men stayed behind.

As you read this story, don't you feel the urgency? I want to reach into the book and grab these cavalier, young men and say, "Fools, get going. You're going to die!"

God often picks us up and gets us out of danger, and we don't always know what the danger might be until much later.

If you are struggling with not wanting to move, consider the larger picture. There might be something treacherous in your path if you stay. Your children might mix with the wrong crowd or your husband's dream job might be deleted. Overwhelming heartaches may insert themselves into your life as a result of staying.

A move isn't always a negative. God may be protecting your whole family, like He tried to protect Lot's family.

Day 11

How low can you go?

We are pressed on every side by troubles, but not crushed and broken. We are perplexed because we don't know why things happen as they do, but we don't give up and quit. We are hunted down, but God never abandons us. We get knocked down, but we get up again and keep going.

II Corinthians 4:8-9 TLB

In the 1960's, my parents would have cookouts on our patio followed by spontaneous after-dinner "make-your-own entertainment." Included in the lineup, my father played his guitar (ála the Kingston Trio), older kids spun hula-hoops, and everyone lined up to do the new dance/game called the Limbo.

The Limbo worked like this: Two volunteers would hold the ends of a three foot bamboo pole, horizontally, waist high. While Caribbean music played, each Limbo participant, one at a time, would bend their body backwards, scooting their legs and bent torso under the pole. Guests would line up to go under the bar and after each turn, the volunteer would lower the bar an inch. If a player touched the bar with their shoulders or chest, they were disqualified.

Now Limbo as a game is great fun. This social icebreaker has people cheering-on their fellow party guests. Unfortunately, limbo in life isn't much of a party game. When we can't sell our house, find a job, or move as we intended, that limbo frustration seeps in.

Bitterness often follows frustration. We ask: Why didn't we sell our house sooner? Why did we put so much money into remodeling the kitchen? Why did my company downsize just when I started?

Life Limbo, as painful as it seems, forces us to look at the bigger picture. Much like the Limbo song asks the player, "How low can you go?" we want to scream, "No lower!" But while standing mid-thigh in life's crises, we realize we can bend more than we imagined. In Limbo-Land we learn to flex our rigid spending habits and, surprisingly, we don't break. We can be happy with less money or a smaller house. We discover how a marriage can weather the unemployment storm with the relationship still intact. Resilience is a quality worth exercising.

I have gone through two years of the Limbo Life. Due to a job change for my husband, we've had a bit of a nomadic life. After going through the gauntlet of anger, depression, self-introspection and apathy, I've finally come out from under the limbo pole. God gave us His game plan a few steps at a time as I stopped fussing and realized He was raising and lowering the bar. I love to keep the bar high so I don't strain while going underneath. But He knows I can bend and become a more flexible disciple for His kingdom.

A life of ease isn't the name of the game when we give our life over to Him, but personal growth is. When we sign up to be disciples of Jesus, we sign on to make our life count for something dearer than comfort.

Whether we are changing zip codes or not, we need to recognize the temporariness of tribulations. Be of good cheer— the "Limbo Dance" won't last forever and we can come out on the other end a different person, more usable and flexible for Jesus.

Day 12

God's favor—more than enough...

It was not by their sword that they won the land, nor did their arm bring them victory; it was your right hand, your arm, and the light of your face, for you loved them.

Psalm 44:3 NIV

On a cool Thanksgiving Day in 1974, David and Susan Cox left their two children with their grandparents in Kokomo, Indiana while they looked for a rental house in Middletown, Ohio. David had just accepted a position and they had an immediate need to find housing.

"We need to be moved here in one week," said David to his wife, shaking his head as he pulled into the parking lot of his new office. "Where are we going to find a rental or a realtor on Thanksgiving Day?" He unlocked the front door and strode over to his desk. He and Susan both plopped down on chairs and started to thumb through the local phone book. It was a stab in the dark but they were desperate for housing. One phone call after another resulted in only voice machines on the other end. Time was short and they had to get something right away.

Finally they got a real person on the line. A realtor had decided to catch up on some work that day, so he was in his office when the Coxes called. Finding someone to help them on a holiday was the first miracle.

"We need a place to rent in less than a week. Would you help us?" they asked.

"Well, I might have one house I could take you to see."

Susan prayed while the two men talked on the phone. She had three desires for a house: an in-ground pool, a fireplace, and no more than $300 a month in rent, a bargain even in the seventies.

A few minutes later the Coxes met the realtor at the house. Susan gasped when she saw the gorgeous backyard pool. As they toured the house they walked down to the basement where a cozy Franklin wood stove/fireplace heated the room—a perfect playroom for their two children.

Holding her breath, she and David inquired about the cost of renting this lovely home. This would be the test to see if the property had their name on it. The realtor looked down at the informational sheet. "Looks like it will rent for three-hundred dollars a month." The Coxes signed the rental agreement a few moments later. They had another miracle.

Who says God doesn't give us our heart's desire? He is our Heavenly Father who graciously blesses us with favor through people. The realtor didn't have to be working that day, but he was. The home didn't have to have a pool and a fireplace, but it did. The rent didn't have to be only $300, but it was.

Today when you pray to your Heavenly Father, remember how He loves to delight His children. Be bold in coming to Him and asking for specific housing needs for your family. He may have the perfect place picked out, but He wants you to trust Him.

Shifting to a New Community

Day 13

The woman of a thousand handshakes...

You shall treat the stranger who sojourns with you as the native among you, and you shall love him as yourself, for you were strangers in the land of Egypt: I am the Lord your God.

Leviticus 19:34 ESV

Can you imagine shaking hands with every new family who moved into your town? Pat Schlitz of Wayne, Illinois remembered how it felt to break into a small community when she moved to a town west of Chicago. Everyone seemed to know each other and Pat didn't see any break in the ice to find friends. Instead of hiding in her house, she came up with a remarkable plan. She introduced herself to every single family that moved in, becoming a one woman Welcome Wagon organization, the organization that used to call on all newcomers. Over a period of years, she greeted 1,000 families, got many women to a community Bible study, and saw changed lives—all because she remembered.

Scripture tells us to befriend strangers who show up in our town. Not only are we to be good neighbors, we are to "love Him as yourself, for you were strangers in the land of Egypt." The New Living Translation says, "Treat them like native-born Israelites." God wanted His people to remember how it felt to be aliens in a foreign land. He wanted them to never forget how the Egyptians made the Hebrews their slaves and overworked them. Many Hebrews built bricks in the hot sun and were beaten when they didn't reach their daily quota. If there was ever any group of people who should have remembered the inhospitality and hostility of a strange land, it was the Israelites.

Can you imagine how churches would flourish if we took this revolutionary attitude of befriending strangers seriously? The front doors of our homes would fling open with coffee invitations, play dates for children, and family barbecue offers. We'd stop talking about our insular lives and turn to the newcomer in our midst to find out about them. I can't imagine a more compelling way to share the good news.

God loves it when we learn from experience because He knows our understanding motivates us to compassion. As we become "old-timers" in our new community, let us never forget the strangers.

Day 14

Not laughing could be a sin...

Our mouths were filled with laughter, our tongues with songs of joy. Then it was said among the nations, "The LORD has done great things for them."

Psalm 126:2 NIV

A cheerful heart is good medicine...

Proverbs 17:22 NLT

Recently, a friend sent me these funny quotes from a church bulletin: "Remember in prayer the many that are sick of our community. Smile at someone who is hard to love. Say 'Hell' to someone who doesn't care much about you."

Pretty funny...but with enough truth to make you think. We who have been in a church community for a while may not realize that some people might be sick of the church. Do we have a reputation of only reporting gloom and doom? Are we convinced people are hard to love when it actually might be that *we* are the one hard to love? When our church community becomes nothing but a cozy bubble, we turn the church into nothing more than a suffocating place where we can complain and use our inside jokes on each other. That comfortable feeling can put up walls for newcomers and a message that says, "Don't bother trying to break into our group."

Christ's community should always be reaching outward. We who have found a new life in Christ should become the most winsome of people. If we reoriented our attitudes and filled them with the Holy Spirit, we might be shocked at how many would like to hear our message. Who wouldn't like to be around happy, joyful people who have a sense of humor? If we offer only deadly, dull, or harried, hyped-up communities of worship, we will be closing the door to those who are searching.

Today, let's not take ourselves and our family so seriously. Chuckle when a teenager says something crazy. Tell a story on yourself. Show the world you are human *and* a Christian. Authenticity is how you show a newcomer the Lord's joy is real. And, if you are struggling to connect to community, don't despair. Throw back your head and laugh. That laughter will open doors to friendship and as an extra bonus, you'll be healthier.

Day 15

That troublesome little verb...

Go then and make disciples of all the nations…

Matthew 28:19 AMP

"Here comes the ice," I hollered over the sound of a buzzing alarm clock as I came banging into my son's room. At sixteen, he had a hard time getting up for a summer factory job and kept oversleeping. Being his mother, I felt it my duty to encourage him by threatening him with uncomfortable consequences for sleeping in, such as pouring a pitcher of water on his motionless body wrapped in a sheet. My threat went unnoticed. He didn't move an inch. Finally, when I upped the ante by plunking a few ice cubes in the pitcher, he decided to divorce himself from his bedcovers and get ready for work. It's a pleasure to see how fast a teenager can move when he or she is spitfire-mad. I only wish I had recorded the moment, full of colorful words and idle threats, for the family album.

I'm a lot like my sleepy son who would not get up. I, too, often want to linger under the bedcovers of my life, comfortable to stay put in my small circle of friends and family. They are the ones who understand my history and are there when things get tough. Unfortunately, when I signed up for the Jesus course, I learned my plans for comfort and understanding didn't always mesh with His. In the book of Matthew, there's one little word that gets in the way of the hunkering down and getting comfortable process. It's the word "go." The passage doesn't read, "Grow roots and make disciples." Oh, how I wish it did. But Jesus propels us to action. We are to get moving to share the good news of the gospel. Instead of surrounding ourselves with loved ones and hoping someone will notice what a happy life we have, Jesus implores us to take the initiative to share out faith.

When He tells us to *go,* the act of doing so is healthy. It shoots us out of our secure world. Too many times we believers surround ourselves with those who say and think as we do— "Pete" and "Repeat." But when we *go,* we put ourselves into locations where we find people who need our Christ community.

You and I can't delete that insistent verb from our life. Whether we go forth in a moving van or just go knock on a neighbor's door, we must always keep that little word at the forefront of all our plans.

Today, ask the Lord if there's any particular place He wants you to *go.*

Day 16

A community of two/ Part 1...

"Don't call me Naomi," she told them. "Call me Mara, because the Almighty has made my life very bitter. I went away full, but the Lord has brought me back empty. Why call me Naomi? The Lord has afflicted me; the Almighty brought misfortune upon me."

Ruth 1:20-21 NIV

The book of Ruth lays out a beautiful story about how God restores family and community. As the story goes, Naomi and her husband moved from Bethlehem to Moab. The country of Moab had been Israel's enemy but now, because of a food shortage in Israel, Naomi and her family had to relocate there. Her two sons wed Moabite women and she started to have the extended family she'd missed in Bethlehem. As time passed, her husband and her two sons died. Naomi, as a good Jewish woman, counted on her husband and subsequently her sons to provide her food and shelter. Unlike today's modern women, she couldn't go out and get a job and be financially independent.

With her family community shattered, she packed up to go to her homeland. Her dreams of having a secure home with plenty of grandchildren running around were gone. Even worse, she wondered how she'd take care of herself.

Have you ever been in a predicament where all the walls

seem to close in around you and there'se no exit sign? Has your family died or left you to fend for yourself? Maybe you are a single mother starting from the beginning as you scratch around to find a house and job to support your children. If so, the story of Ruth and Naomi will give you reassurance as you move to another location. Naomi started to become bitter to the point where she changed her name to "Bitter" (Mara). If she had been living today she might have even been on medication for depression. She had no social security or pension, no IRA or money market account. Her security was family and it was gone.

Naomi had to learn to lean on God for her security. As she went back to Bethlehem, she started getting back her confidence in God as she remembered a relative who might help her. But it took hitting the bottom of the well before she found her community first in God.

Are you about to hit the bottom of the well? You can learn from Naomi's life how God supplies every need in unusual ways.

Day 17

A community of two/ Part 2...

So Boaz took Ruth and she became his wife. When they came together, the LORD made her conceive, and she bore a son. Then the women said to Naomi, "Blessed be the LORD, who has not left you this day without next-of-kin; and may his name be renowned in Israel! He shall be to you a restorer of life and a nourisher of your old age; for your daughter-in-law who loves you, who is more to you than seven sons, has borne him." Then Naomi took the child and laid him in her bosom, and became his nurse. The women of the neighborhood gave him a name, saying, "A son has been born to Naomi." They named him Obed; he became the father of Jesse, the father of David.

Ruth 4:13-17 NRSV

*N*aomi had to learn to lean on God for her security. As she went back to Bethlehem, she started getting back her confidence in her Creator. Using the Jewish law of redeemed kinsman, she remembered a relative who was qualified to marry her daughter-in-law. Shrewdly, she directed Ruth to work in this relative's field, gleaning for grain.

As was the custom, landowners allowed poor widows and orphans to follow the workers and gather any grain they left behind. Soon, Ruth had favor with the relative, Boaz, as he insisted the workers make sure she had plenty to take home.

As the story unfolds, one night Ruth presented herself as available for marriage by sleeping at the foot of Boaz's bed.

Ruth followed her mother-in-law to a new country without any promise of a stable life. But God, always directing behind the scenes, brought this foreigner a new husband as she learned to trust in Jehovah. He gave her not only a new husband, but a whole new community of faith. And because of her obedience, she was grafted into the family of Jesse and into the lineage of the coming Savior, Jesus.

Day 18

Fourth-grade recess...

He who despises his neighbor sins, but blessed is he who is kind to the needy.

Proverbs 14:21 NIV

When you're a new girl in fourth-grade you fall into the "needy" category. I won't ever forget Jo Ann Borgbreen. She moved into our town and school shortly after the start of the fourth grade. Pale-skinned and taller than the rest of us, she stood out in the class. She had long skinny legs which were covered with calamine lotion. I guess I wasn't the only one who noticed she stuck out; she didn't get the friendliest reception in Mrs. Morse's class.

Jo Ann stood at the monkey bars until one of us gave her the okay to join us. It was back in the days when girls wore dresses to school and in spite of our big, full, "twirly" skirts, we all played on the monkey bars at recess. It didn't take long before some of the boys started hanging around the playground. My perceptive 10-year-old mind knew something was up. Sure enough, a few lunch breaks later rumors flew: "The new girl has yellow underpants and you know what that means!"

Now you know there's nothing punkier than fourth-grade boys. Jo Ann had a crummy, undeserved reputation before her parents even came to the back-to-school open house. Honestly, the only thing wrong with her was she had this chalky, pink lotion on her legs. I felt sorry for her. A couple of us decided to be friendly to her and invited her to play jacks (yes, I said jacks—look it up in your history book) on the cement walkway. She turned out to be a great friend. Just goes to show—never trust a fourth-grade boy.

Being the new kid isn't easy.

Today, if you have children and you are fortunate to be settled, teach them to look out for the new kids. Going to a new school can traumatize a child. But having even one friend to hold your hand at recess or choose you to be their science project partner can make all the difference. Children can learn at an early age to reach out and be God's light to a scared little classmate. I know because as a mother I've been on the receiving end of such kindness to my family.

Your kids can learn early that creating community starts with them.

Day 19

Brief encounters = eternal results...

Paul then stood up in the meeting of the Areopagus and said: "Men of Athens! I see that in every way you are very religious. For as I walked around and looked carefully at your objects of worship, I even found an altar with this inscription: TO AN UNKNOWN GOD. Now what you worship as something unknown I am going to proclaim to you.

The God who made the world and everything in it is the Lord of heaven and earth and does not live in temples built by hands. And he is not served by human hands, as if he needed anything, because he himself gives all men life and breath and everything else. From one man he made every nation of men that they should inhabit the whole earth; and he determined the times set for them and the exact places where they should live. God did this so that men would seek him and perhaps reach out for him and find him, though he is not far from each one of us. 'For in him we live and move and have our being.' As some of your own poets have said, 'We are his offspring.'

Therefore since we are God's offspring, we should not think that the divine being is like gold or silver or stone—an image made by man's design and skill. In the past God overlooked such ignorance, but now he commands all people everywhere to repent. For he has set a day when he will judge the world with justice by the man he has appointed. He has given proof of this to all men by raising him from the dead."

When they heard about the resurrection of the dead, some of them sneered, but others said, "We want to hear you again on this subject."

Acts 17:22-32 NIV

I noticed her shoes first. As I sat down at the coffee bar in Barnes & Noble, my eyes caught a pair of red felt elf boots with upturned toes. I commented to the owner on her unusual footwear and she commented on my reading material, the Bible. We chatted for a few minutes and the topic soon turned to deeper things.

"I can't really believe in a loving God if He is like my father. He's quite controlling," she stated.

"Yes, some of us can't use our human fathers as an example, but having a flawed parent doesn't rule out the kindness of God," I explained. After a few minutes we exchanged emails. I met with this questioning college student a couple more times before I had to move away.

It was a chance encounter in a city where my husband and I lived for just a few short months. Not having a full time job, I'd show up at a public place and pray for opportunities to show God's love. As I parked myself at a coffee shop or on an outdoor bench, I became fascinated by those God brought across my path. He taught me the concept of planting myself somewhere in the midst of people and seeing what happens.

The apostle Paul planted himself smack dab in the middle of a hill in Athens called Mars Hill. This hill was a gathering place for the local philosophers. Epicureans who felt life was for seeking pleasure and Stoics whose philosophy was to live above any emotion in life, battled it out in public. Paul used this meeting place to speak to both sides, referring to their statue of the unknown god. He proclaimed how all could know the name of the unknown god. His name was Jesus.

Always on the move, he traveled from city to city spending nights in many new believers' homes. As a man focused on his goal, he kept his eyes alert for all opportunities to preach Christ.

You and I, like Paul, may find ourselves in temporary quarters. We may be waiting for a house to sell or we might be in the armed services with a career that requires moving every couple of years to another military base. If we observe Paul's life, we notice his gift for redeeming his time in whatever town he was in, for as short a period as he might have had.

Take advantage of those "temporary" moves and use that transitory time to bless others. All time periods are temporary in light of eternity.

A challenge: If you had to move today, would you have accomplished all that He wanted you to accomplish in your current place of residence?

Day 20

Are you in the rear?

As soon as they had brought them out, one of them said, "Flee for your lives! Don't look back, and don't stop anywhere in the plain! Flee to the mountains or you will be swept away!" But Lot said to them, "No, my lords, please! Your servant has found favor in your eyes, and you have shown great kindness to me in sparing my life. But I can't flee to the mountains; this disaster will overtake me, and I'll die. Look, here is a town near enough to run to, and it is small. Let me flee to it–it is very small, isn't it? Then my life will be spared."

He said to him, "Very well, I will grant this request too; I will not overthrow the town you speak of. But flee there quickly, because I cannot do anything until you reach it." (That is why the town was called Zoar).

By the time Lot reached Zoar, the sun had risen over the land. Then the LORD rained down burning sulfur on Sodom and Gomorrah—from the LORD out of the heavens. Thus he overthrew those cities and the entire plain, destroying all those living in the cities – and also the vegetation in the land. But Lot's wife looked back, and she became a pillar of salt.

Genesis 19:17-26 NIV

"Don't look back," she was warned, not by her husband, but by powerful angels. And yet, a nagging desire persisted and she turned her head. She had to have that final view. The word for "to look" in this portion of scripture means more than a peek at something. The Hebrew word for "looking back," means to pay attention to, regard or consider.

We might assume when Lot's wife took that second glance, it was to yearn for all she had left. In spite of the corrupt society where she and Lot raised their children, she seemed to yearn for her home. Later on in the passage she turns into a pillar or a "*natsiyb,*" which "refers to a garrison or a deputy, something set to watch over something else." To this day, she stands permanently guarding the Dead Sea.

The story of Lot's wife is one of the more eerie passages in the Old Testament. One wonders why she minded leaving. Maybe she was so entrenched in her neighborhood, clubs, organizations, PTO, favorite grocery store, and seamstress that she couldn't imagine living anywhere else. It really makes one stop and wonder how someone could be so blind to the evil surrounding their family.

Are you struggling with a move, lagging behind your spouse and the rest of the family? Are you in the rear, conjuring up nostalgic memories when you should be at the head of the line? Life is too short for clinging to the past. Today, let's cut loose those past memories of the perfect home you used to have. A perfect home is where your family dwells.

Lot's wife reminds us to keep moving forward to heed God's

call. In Luke 9:62, Jesus Himself exhorted a man to put his hand to the plow and not look back. Wishing for something we used to have is foolish. Just ask Lot's daughters.

Day 21

Securing the security code...

The LORD will keep you from all harm—he will watch over your life; the LORD will watch over your coming and going both now and forevermore.

Psalm 121:7-8 NIV

The police cruiser pulled up to the curb. I stood in the hallway clad in my bathrobe while my husband opened the door to the local police in our new town.

Great way to make an impression on the neighbors, I thought.

"False alarm," my husband said sheepishly explaining how we had just moved in and didn't know how to operate the security system. Most likely the old owners had the instruction book and security code ensconced on the bottom of one of their boxes on the way to Texas. We thanked the officers and closed the front door, laughing. We certainly had announced our arrival.

In the Psalms we are told of God's promise to watch our comings and goings in life. Biblical characters faced attacks from neighboring countries, famine, and loneliness when God called them to move to their next home. They didn't know what marauding tribe they'd run into over the next mountain. They had no option but to hang onto God's word as they traveled to unknown territories.

As a FM (Frequent Mover), I have camped out on this verse,

holding on to His ability to protect us. Often as a young mother I'd be alone in a new city with three little children. I remember one time in particular when we moved to Strongsville, Ohio. My husband flew a lot as a national sales manager for his company and because we had three small children, I needed good neighbors. When we moved, I often fought fear, wondering how I'd cope with a potential crisis while my husband was several states away. I knew no one and our family lived three-hundred miles away. But before we had moved, we diligently prayed to be put in the right neighborhood. Within a week, women on each side of our home asked me to coffee and helped when my eighteen-month-old daughter locked the boys and myself out of our house.

Maybe you know the security code for your new home but you're concerned of never finding a good doctor, church, or a great school for your children. Let's challenge ourselves to trust the fact that He's gone ahead to prepare the way in our new place. He will guard our emotions as we walk through that unfamiliar front door. He knows the exact security code to guard our heart from fear.

Day 22

The dangerous job of sheep herding...

Go rather to the lost sheep of Israel. As you go, proclaim this message: "The kingdom of heaven is near."

Matthew 10:6-7 NIV

*D*id you ever think of a move as God's catapulting you out to another mission field? As newlyweds, my husband and I attended a dynamic church in California before we moved to the Midwest. Brimming with hope and enthusiasm for our new city, we tried different churches. Finally we settled into a smaller church in the same denomination in which my husband grew up. We had hoped for close fellowship. Instead, we discovered strife and disharmony between the pastor and the assistant pastor. In addition, it appeared newcomers were a threat to the assistant pastor's wife who seemed to work behind the scenes to make sure we weren't welcome.

We didn't have an agenda with the new church other than to make friends. I had left my family out in California and as a new mother with a preemie newborn, I craved fellowship. But by placing us in the crossfire of a divided church, God used our presence to root out some ugly divisions.

We didn't plan to step into a spiritual war zone, but in

Matthew 10:6-7 it's apparent He sends some to "preach to the lost sheep of Israel." Lost sheep often want to be lost, but God still uses His people to call them back. He may send *us* to help prod lost sheep out of the ditch and back into grazing meadows.

We are called to be ministers of the Gospel. We aren't necessarily called to a life of spiritual ease. Today I challenge all of us to look around and see if He might be calling us to strengthen a failing church where lost sheep are running rampant. Rebuilding a church the enemy has bombed honors God in a special way even if we have to dodge a few sheep hoof grenades.

Day 23

What...company again?

Offer hospitality to one another without grumbling.

I Peter 4:9 NIV

I grew up in a hospitable home. Over the years my parents hosted five exchange students, a foster child with learning disabilities, and a random Swedish maid my father found crying in a parking lot and brought home to dinner. Grandparents came and went, along with an aunt who always brought us handmade puppets and homemade strawberry jam. My three siblings and I had lots of slumber parties and friends over to dinner. We thought nothing of having visitors. We'd just plop another sleeping bag down on the living room rug and my father would make extra chocolate chip pancake batter in the morning. Visitors and guests were the norm. It made life exciting.

Unfortunately, practicing hospitality has become a victim to overbooked schedules. Even the Welcome Wagon organization doesn't make house calls anymore, but prefers to greet you through the World Wide Web. So, what's a new family to do to find community?

Throw a party...any party. Yes, I know you wish someone would knock on your door with a bouquet of daisies, but get over it. Remember, the Bible tells us not to grumble. If you want to meet people, you will have to be the initiator and the best time is right when you move. I had every woman on my street over for Christmas brunch when I first moved to Zionsville, Indiana. There's no better time to entertain than when you have a legitimate excuse not to clean because you, are surrounded by boxes.

Choose what works for you but make it small and simple:
- Coffee and donuts
- A pot of soup or chili for two nearby families
- Ice cream sundaes for all the neighborhood children
- Popcorn, soda, and a DVD
- A Mary Kay, Pampered Chef, or Arbonne product party

Even if you never get another invitation back, you've started breaking into the community. Let's challenge ourselves to plan one simple event for either the adults or children in the neighborhood. Write down ideas that would work and put a date on your calendar. You won't regret it.

Day 24

No roots...

Jesus said, "My kingdom is not of this world. If it were, my servants would fight to prevent my arrest by the Jews. But now my kingdom is from another place."

John 18:36 NIV

I once asked Muriel Cook, counselor-at-large for the Multnomah School of the Bible, what she considered a woman's greatest need. I thought she'd say love or family. Instead, she told me how studies cite security as a woman's biggest concern. A woman can withstand a lot of turmoil if she knows her life has protected walls around it. A loyal husband, supportive friends, and a "nest" with all her favorite furnishings gives a woman a sense of well-being.

Men and women both need a home, but Jesus never had that security. The Bible is filled with ironies and one of the greatest is in the book of Luke. When Jesus sent out disciples to Samaria, He Himself prepared to head to Jerusalem. The disciples were given a cool reception—they realized they been brushed off. James and John, probably angered because they, Jewish followers of Christ who had reached out to their enemies, cried, "Revenge."

Jesus was heading into the final phase of His ministry and would not be on the earth much longer. Maybe He shook His head as he thought of the wonderful creation He had made, while

He, Himself, had no home. He who had created the broom tree under which Elijah slept and the cave where David hid, could not Himself find a place to lay his head at night. No, He knew His kingdom was elsewhere.

Maybe you are feeling the insecurity of adjusting to a new home. Old friends you could always depend upon are miles away. Your new kitchen is too small, the rooms too dark. Familiar routines are broken as you force yourself to develop new ones. The Bible reminds us we, too, have no true home on earth.

I find comfort in the transient life of Jesus. He never dug in His heels and said, "I'll operate from this office." Instead, He traveled about meeting the needs of the people. If we can refocus our jittery emotions and find our home and security in Him, we will be free to move forward and meet the exciting challenges we find in our new community. Our challenge today is to relinquish our desire for security and find ourselves at home in Jesus.

Day 25

Stuck in the quicksand...

I waited patiently for the LORD; he turned to me and heard my cry. He lifted me out of the slimy pit, out of the mud and mire; he set my feet on a rock and gave me a firm place to stand. He put a new song in my mouth, a hymn of praise to our God. Many will see and fear and put their trust in the LORD.

Psalm 40:1-3 NIV

My family and I used to spend a few summer weeks at a Michigan cottage near beautiful Lake Ann. To look at the lake, you'd see nothing but placid water waiting to be stroked with a paddle. What the average city slicker can't see is a hidden danger back in the swampy area. Where cattails and water lilies warn of shallow waters, where the creek feeds the lake, you'll find the bottom of the lake made of quicksand. From the little I've heard about quicksand, I know the more you struggle to pull yourself out the deeper you go. On that quiet part of the lake where boaters rarely sail by, one might be stuck indefinitely. We stayed away not wanting to experience that particular adventure.

King David, who wrote many of the Psalms, talks about the slimy pit. It may not have been quicksand, but something just as terrifying that grabbed him, sucking him down. David knew what it was like to live by the seat of his pants as Saul, the evil king of Israel, continually pursued him. He moved from place to place, living in fields or caves. For years David didn't have a place to call his own.

Maybe you've had to move a lot and where you currently live feels unstable or transient. Perhaps you've lost your support group and now you slip and slide to connect with your new community. The Bible reminds us how God will lift us out of a slimy pit. He has promised to rescue us and when He does, He puts us on firm ground—a solid rock. Finally, the psalmist tells us that God puts a new song in our mouth, a song with our new address.

I encourage anyone struggling with settling into an unfamiliar community to remember these promises. It will happen. Look forward to being on firm ground again and singing a new song with your new address.

Day 26

Kitchen windows...

For now we see through a glass, darkly; but then face to face: now I know in part; but then shall I know even as also I am known.

I Corinthians: 13:12 KJV

I'd love to line up all the kitchen window views I've ever had. I started my journey looking out onto a college apartment balcony with a view of a dreary cement wall and a wooden railing with peeling paint. After getting married and moving to the Sierra Nevada Mountains, I fixed coffee while watching chipmunks scamper up and down the twenty-foot tall boulders in the backyard. When we moved to the Midwest, I could view my children playing on a swing set surrounded by a lush green lawn. Chicago brought a postage-stamp yard and a side porch I viewed from a window adjacent to the kitchen. Now in North Carolina we've put out a bird feeder and I enjoy scarlet cardinals and flamboyant yellow goldfinches fighting over their breakfast.

My kitchen views sum up my life. Each place had its season for me as a newlywed, new mother, veteran mother of four and, finally, circling again back to life with just my husband. My album of windows reminds me how quickly life passes. In the first kitchen I learned how to cook basic dishes and how not to burn pans. Later, I'd spend hours making baby food. Hearty casseroles for a family of six soon replaced the baby food. And finally, I substituted the casseroles devoured by starving teenagers for smaller intimate meals for just my husband and myself.

Many views—many places—one existence. He is the one who has pieced all my moves into one steady life. I never thought I'd move a lot. I lived in the same house on the same street from age five until college. God had a different plan for my grown-up years. And I thank Him for each window through which I've been privileged to view the world.

Have you ever seen your life through different windows? Different doors? What did you see? What has God taught you in each location? What kind of community waits outside your window?

Day 27

Southern-fried speaking...

Why don't you understand the language I use? Is it because you can't understand the words I use?

John 8:43 God's Word Translation

"Call the police."

Now I can panic a bit, but when the oil-change attendant waved for me to pull up and said, "Call the police," I hesitated. Did I hear him right? I whipped out my cell phone assuming the previous customer just drove off without payment. Of course I'd be happy to nab that greedy driver who's not paying and making the bill higher for the rest of us. I rolled down my window to talk to the young employee.

"Looks like someone drove off without paying. Or maybe worse, but I figured you look pretty calm for having just been robbed."

The man shot me a confused look.

Now I was puzzled. "Didn't you just ask me to call the police?"

"No, ma'am, I just said, 'Pull up please.'"

I could almost hear his thoughts: "Dumb Yankee...can't even understand English!"

I'm afraid I had to agree.

Sometimes it seems like God's plans for us are also lost in

translation. It's as if He is speaking Japanese to us and we just haven't learned the lesson. Should we move here or stay put? Should we put our children in public school or home-school them? How large a mortgage should we bite off? All these questions are important and we want to hear God's will for our lives. But fretting seems to keep us from hearing what He wants for us.

As you and I adjust to a move, we need to remember that God wants to communicate with us. James 1:5 tells us that if we lack wisdom, we should ask God for it and He will give it to us generously. It might take time to translate into your circumstances, but we serve a God who loves to translate his truth into our lives. Today, believe that whatever decisions you are wrestling with, He will have an answer.

Day 28

Finding second chances in a Dutch oven...

Simon Peter said to him, "Lord, where are you going?" Jesus answered, "Where I am going, you cannot follow me now; but you will follow afterward." Peter said to him, "Lord, why can I not follow you now? I will lay down my life for you." Jesus answered, "Will you lay down your life for me? Very truly, I tell you, before the cock crows, you will have denied me three times.

John 13:36-38 NRSV

And I tell you that you are Peter, and on this rock I will build my church, and the gates of Hades will not overcome it.

Matthew 16:18 NIV

It arrived on my doorstep. Inside I discovered a sturdy box from my favorite cookware company. Sawing open the container to free the pot, I realized I had a brand new replacement for the Dutch oven I had burned and sent to be repaired. I expected a large bill to fix it, but fortunately for me, the bottom of the pan was irreparable so the company sent me, a brand new one. I, the ever-forgetful chef, had destroyed an indestructible piece of cookware while making chili and deserved to pay a hefty repair bill. Instead, UPS delivered a brand new replacement—grace in a Dutch oven. The shiny red enamel cookware perches on my stovetop as a reminder of second chances.

The disciple Peter, in all his impulsive enthusiasm, insisted he would lay down his life for Jesus. Instead, he denied knowing Christ three times. Not once, not twice, but three times. If anyone wanted to rewind their life and get a second crack at it, I'm sure it was Peter. We can't even imagine the self-loathing he must have gone through after turning his back on his savior. Yet God, in His grace, gave Peter a chance to not only redeem himself, but to become the foundation of the early church.

Moving gives us second chances. Yes, there are many downsides to moving, but one of the greatest advantage is getting a fresh start in a new community. Just like my unblemished new cookware with its creamy white inside and rosy red outside, there are endless opportunities in a new place to begin again. No one knows we got fired at our last job, our kids were naughty at recess, and our yard was full of weeds. In a new location we can leave past failures behind. If Peter could, so can we.

Let's challenge each other to put our best foot forward today. When we go to the grocery store, apply for a job, or meet a neighbor, we are a fresh page. We have many chances to make lasting first impressions. If we keep our minds open, we may find this new location one of the best.

Day 29

Remember...

My soul is downcast within me; therefore I will remember you from the land of the Jordan,
the heights of Hermon—from Mount Mizar.
Deep calls to deep in the roar of your waterfalls; all your waves and breakers have swept over me.
By day the LORD directs his love, at night his song is with me—a prayer to the God of my life.
I say to God my Rock, "Why have you forgotten me? Why must I go about mourning, oppressed by the enemy?"
My bones suffer mortal agony as my foes taunt me, saying to me all day long, "Where is your God?"
Why, my soul, are you downcast? Why so disturbed within me? Put your hope in God, for I will yet praise him, my Savior and my God."

Psalm 42:6-11 NIV

Sometimes right before or after a move, I know I will need a good talking-to. After saying goodbye to dear friends, I feel pangs of loneliness. I need to catch my mind before it takes off for the outer limits of self-pity, a very sad land. I will sit down and tell my brain to behave and stop going off the deep end. Emotions are funny that way; we need to corral them before they take charge of our lives.

Read King David's words. David always had trouble—woman trouble, political trouble, and lots of children trouble. At one point he had King Saul hunting him for the kill. But David had learned how to call upon God from the depths of despair. He starts out the sixth verse feeling downcast and forlorn. But true to David's writings, by the end of the Psalm he is praising God. He ends with, "Put your hope in God for I will yet praise him, my Savior and my God."

Just like King David, we can each remember God from places we have lived and know He has always met us with fellowship. He is the rock from where we build our community.

Day 30

A secure home...

He who fears the Lord has a secure fortress, and for his children it will be a refuge. The fear of the Lord is a fountain of life, turning a man from the snares of death.

Proverbs 14:26- 27 NIV

"Rapist," the news anchor blared out. "Be on the lookout."

I clicked off the television and doubled checked the locks on the patio door before going to bed. But my brain didn't retire. It didn't help that I'd just watched the movie of the week where a woman had experienced the same kind of break-in. My vivid imagination kept me tossing and turning in bed. I thought we'd moved to a safe community. It was okay when my husband was at home, but lately he'd been traveling more and with two little kids to protect from a potential intruder, I was frightened.

There's no completely safe community anywhere. We hear of meth dealers hiding out in little towns or high up in mountain resorts. Kids in suburban schools go on shooting rampages or plant bombs in restrooms. Big cities have their share of gang problems. But as Proverbs says, the Lord offers a secure fortress. According to the Encarta Dictionary, fortress means "a fortified place with a long-term military presence, or something that acts as protection."

If you and I find ourselves in a new community, this verse

in Proverbs should comfort us. You may have to spend some nights alone if your husband has a business trip, but what a wonderful promise God has given us. We need to understand God's powerful ability to send angels to keep us safe. Our job is to believe that and as we do, we calm our children's fears, as well as our own.

Do you have any fears about living in your new community? Just remember that our God has given us a refuge. Claim His promise of protection.

Day 31

Culture shock...

Though I am free and belong to no man, I make myself a slave to everyone, to win as many as possible. To the Jews I became like a Jew, to win the Jews. To those under the law I became like one under the law (though I myself am not under the law), so as to win those under the law. To those not having the law I became like one not having the law (though I am not free from God's law but am under Christ's law), so as to win those not having the law. To the weak I became weak, to win the weak. I have become all things to all men so that by all possible means I might save some. I do all this for the sake of the gospel, that I may share in its blessings.

1 Corinthians 9:19-23 NIV

I once overheard a gentleman from Mississippi talking about the differences between how Southerners and Northerners conduct business. He used an example of a Chicago dealer who would call him up to inquire about an order. The conversation went something like this:

Northerner: "Hey Joe, I've got three customers on my back and I need my shipment ASAP. When do you think I can get it? Let me know because one of the customers is really pushing me."

The Southern gentleman then explained why this wasn't the way you did business in the lower half of the country. He explained: "The first thing you do when you talk to a business associate is inquire about his family. 'How's the wife? Is your son still on the football team? Have you seen that new grandbaby yet?' Even if you don't know the person well, you still go through the pleasantries before beginning any business discussion." He explained that it appears rude to just start in on a business issue before running through the preliminaries.

Now, a Northerner listening to the conversation might say, "Get to the point. I am calling about a problem and I'm short on time. I'm not being rude, but I needed an answer yesterday. Quit dilly-dallying around with non-business conversations." Efficiency drives his discussions.

You have just seen an example of two different cultures in action. Neither is wrong, but it's helpful to understand another culture in order to have success in a community. In one area of the country where we lived, no one ever cut grass on Sunday and we honored that community standard. In another area, we learned it was important to wave to every neighbor passing by so they wouldn't think we were stuck-up. In other neighborhoods, people thought waving was weird.

As you seek community in a new location, pay attention to Paul's words. Paul devoted his life to understanding the culture of the churches he started. In some places he started his ministry in a synagogue. In others, the local meeting place. When we can adapt to the local traditions, we will have a greater chance to build community.

Day 32

Last man standing...

He (Elijah) *replied, "I have been very zealous for the LORD God Almighty. The Israelites have rejected your covenant, broken down your altars, and put your prophets to death with the sword. I am the only one left, and now they are trying to kill me too."*

1 Kings 19:10 NIV

"Wow, they sure don't like Christians here," my friend's daughter proclaimed after the first week in her new high school. "I think I'm the only believer."

Some moves make us feel like we've slipped into enemy territory. Maybe our new town offers few dynamic churches. Or maybe the locals love to label Christians as "right-wingers" and shoot editorial darts in the newspaper. It's hard to adjust when we've previously experienced a surplus of fellowship and encouragement in a place where many knew our children and our history. The natural impulse in an unfriendly town is to lock the front door, close the blinds, and mourn the fact that we are misunderstood— hoping the Rapture will take us out of this foreign territory.

Elijah the prophet felt very alone after coming off one of the largest group miracles in his life. He had confronted the prophets of Baal with a showdown of their gods versus the God of Israel. On top of Mount Carmel he gave the Israelites a chance to choose the true God, but only silence answered his plea. Of course, after God consumed Elijah's sacrifice, Israel chose to serve the living God. But Elijah knew the fickleness of his people as he wondered how long the commitment would last.

Charging down Mount Carmel after his success, Elijah found the wicked Queen Jezebel vowing to murder him. He slipped into depression. Under a broom tree in the desert, he told God he was the *only* one serving Him. God revealed how 7,000 others had *not* bowed to the god of Baal.

God might take us from a place of prestige where we are mayor of our town to a city where we feel disliked and misunderstood. He's not as interested in our soft little comfort zones as He is with us learning to trust Him anywhere.

A woman who had just moved from the from the South to the North told her family, "God is bigger than Tennessee." Well said. God's people are everywhere, but more important, so is He. He will meet us in every new place, even under a broom tree in the desert. Our challenge today is to pray for one good friend. His church is everywhere.

Day 33

Love your enemies—even your neighbors...

...But I tell you: Love your enemies and pray for those who persecute you.

Matthew 5:44 NIV

An old Gaelic blessing goes like this: "May those who love us, love us. And those that don't love us, love us. May God turn their hearts and if He doesn't turn their hearts, may He turn their ankle so we will know them by their limping."

When I read this I laughed out loud. People want to be admired, esteemed, and loved. It's part of our DNA. It's also part of our make-up to want a little something rotten to happen to those who don't appreciate us. We may not want to see our enemies mortally wounded, but a minor injury might be okay.

The problem is, if we have pitched our tent under God's graceful sky, we are exhorted to love our neighbors. Part of moving is adjusting to new people around us. For most of my moves, I have had great neighbors. But I do remember one family I struggled to love. They had several children who behaved like angels until the parents went out. Then magically, as the parents' minivan backed out of the driveway, these little darlings grew horns. My most vivid recollection is of the oldest boy taking a rubber sling, putting a water balloon in it, and slamming it against our house as he yelled uncomplimentary things about our family. Now, if you sling these water-logged missiles several times into an aluminum-sided wall, they can leave quite a few dents. *Grrr!* Our home value dropped drastically in one afternoon. I won't deny I wished for a few sprained ankles on that family.

Whoever said we'd have an easy life as Christians? Some of the little irritations sure steal our joy. But as the family next door becomes sandpaper to our rough emotions, we learn to speak the truth in love while still keeping out the welcome mat.

Day 34

Hey—I'm here...

I stand up in the assembly and cry for help.
Job 30:28b NIV

Maybe it was because my dog had just died, or that I only saw my husband on weekends. But living in a new city with my grown children miles away, I guess I sort of cracked that Wednesday morning at church.

The sweet Bible study leader passed around the written pray request basket. Being a bit of a rebel, I asked if I could speak my prayer request. With a short hesitation, she nodded. Maybe she had a premonition I was about to launch a verbal avalanche.

I gulped and started in, "You're all very nice Christian women and I am enjoying the study, but I need to tell you, I'm lonely. I'm new in town. I can't find a job and my husband flies all around the country so I don't see him until the weekend. I need someone to talk to or a friend to go with me for coffee." I paused a moment. "And please don't all call tonight because you feel guilty about what I've said."

I could hear the Metra train racing by outside the window, a clock ticking in the other room, and several women around me sucking in their breath. It was an awkward, but needed, moment.

I've learned in life how sometimes you and I just need to pull back the tent flap and let people see what's going on inside the tent. We may have to announce we are hurting and a little help would be appreciated. Poor Job, with his miserably judgmental friends, certainly needed someone to give him comfort. Can't you just hear him at the city gate as he called out in a scratchy little whimper seeking someone who could understand his predicament?

Maybe you're in the place where I was; visiting a church but not yet connected. You probably won't have to erupt in public, but if you can find a kind soul to confide in, please do. People are busy and sometimes don't mean to neglect newcomers, but it happens. Don't take it personally, but find that person with a listening ear and a craving for a caramel latte.

Day 35

Attacking anxiety...

Peace I leave with you; my peace I give you. I do not give to you as the world gives. Do not let your hearts be troubled and do not be afraid.

John 14:27 NIV

I am blonde by choice, but ditzy blonde by nature. When I started having dizzy spells in stores, I knew it was more than my spacey thinking. One day at the drugstore while standing by the toothpaste section, I felt I had to get out of the store or a sales clerk would trip over me in the aisle. Fleeing the store, I hopped into my car but was too light-headed to drive. After a few minutes, my head cleared and I aimed the car toward home.

These intermittent episodes came out of nowhere and scared me until I realized I was experiencing an anxiety attack. When I thought about it, it seemed reasonable. Within two years we had lived in two temporary apartments (planning our daughter's wedding in one of them), moved back to Michigan, sold that home, and then moved to Chicago. My body declared I had reached my stress limit.

For several years I still battled fear, wondering when the wicked dart would show up in my life again. Would I be driving on the highway to visit my daughter or at a backyard barbecue where I visited with friends? Would I have to leave suddenly? The good news is the enemy didn't win.

Our enemy wants us to think he has supreme power to torture. The truth is he is a liar. Yes, we all go through times of struggle, but we can still have peace in our lives. When I understood what I was fighting against, I pulled out God's powerful weapons of mass destruction—scripture. Result: the beginnings of victory.

Moving can take a toll on our body, but when we fight the slings and arrows of the enemy, we see God's power at work. If you are exhausted and your body isn't coping well with your new move, take deep breaths from your diaphragm. Tell yourself this is a natural way the body copes with stress. And remember… you will experience relief even while fighting the enemy, and your life will get back to normal—soon.

Day 36

Crack-patchers' gospel...

Then the master told his servant, "Go out to the roads and country lanes and make them come in, so that my house will be full."

Luke 14:23 NIV

It started with a mailbox. My family and I had moved from a large community to a new house in a smaller Midwestern town. The new subdivision, Hunter Green, was complete except for the finishing touches—mailboxes. The builder told us to purchase generic mailboxes until the permanent designer mailboxes arrived from the manufacturer.

A month later they arrived, all a standard size and decorated with wild birds. Sandy Schmitt, another newcomer, ignored the edict to install her new box. She liked her personalized dinosaur one, appropriate for a former Smithsonian Institution archeologist.

From this, a small controversy began percolating. Matching wild bird mailboxes were a high priority in this subdivision. Tongues clucked, but evidently Sandy wasn't going to conform. Intrigued, I knocked on her door to meet this rugged suburban individual. As we sipped coffee, I discovered she hadn't grown up locally. Sandy, like me, hailed from out West. While she showed me her flowerbed mix of eccentric wildflowers, I thought of the proper petunias and marigolds planted in other front yards.

This gal's not a cookie-cutter homemaker. She'll shake things up.

Halloween arrived and many hung tasteful autumn sprays on their front doors. Sandy, however, displayed an outrageous collection of witches and wizards on her lawn. Goblins and devils shrieked through the loudspeaker on her porch along with R.I.P. tombstones of her family. I could hear the neighbors whisper, "Outrageous."

One woman took up the challenge to put Sandy on notice. She marched up to the front door, her righteous speech on the tip of her tongue. Sandy, thinking someone had finally welcomed her to the neighborhood, threw open the door with friendly anticipation. No such luck. The woman, Bible in hand instead of a pan of welcoming brownies, notified Sandy of her inappropriate and very offensive decorations.

Sandy looked puzzled as she relayed the incident to me. In her ignorance goblins and demons represented fairy-tale fun. She asked, "Why would anyone care how I decorate my lawn?"

The *Christian Cringe Alarm* went off in my head while I listened—Pharisee alert. What gopher hole could I hide in? Actually the only yard with a gopher was my own. No, I didn't favor celebrating ghouls, but I felt ashamed of the women who condemned this neighbor.

That's what made me decide to be a Crack-patcher in Sandy's

life. I determined to befriend her. We roller-bladed. We took our kids to the park. While our daughters played dress-up, I offered suggestions for a good pediatrician and admired her extensive vegetable garden.

When spiritual topics came up, I kept things low-key. Other than a few references to answered prayer, I just tried to be a friend. In some ways I had more in common with her than the women at church. Living in this tight-knit community, I, too, had "come late to the party." Even though I broke the ice with many neighbors and made several acquaintances, I had two definite advantages over Sandy. I had the correct mailbox... and I attended church. Sandy, shunned like a pagan leper, didn't seem to notice the snubs. But I did.

After another move across town I saw less of Sandy. Busy families kept our paths from crossing. When the phone rang one night after dinner, I was surprised to hear her voice.

"I know you are kind of a religious person so I thought I'd call you."

"What's up?" I inquired.

She paused before choking up. "It's my father-in-law. He's been diagnosed with cancer."

"I'm so sorry," I replied.

"Well, I know you pray and so I was wondering if you'd pray for him."

Years have passed since my friendship with Sandy. We've both moved out of state. But I grin when I remember the rebel of Hunter Green subdivision. Sandy taught me a lot about reaching out to people. God puts certain people in our lives for a reason. Through Sandy, God taught me to choose friendship over neighborhood approval. And I continue to hear the quiet voice of God saying, "Pay attention to life's cracks. You need to be there to pull people out and patch up those cracks."

Is there someone you know who is being ignored because he or she doesn't fit in? As ambassadors of Christ we need to be the first person to extend a hand of friendship. Look around and see if you can find someone who doesn't have community. You and I can be the person to bring them friendship and share the love of Christ.

Day 37

Neighbor hall of fame...

Don't look out only for your own interests, but take an interest in others, too.

Philippians 2:4 NLT

I have had some terrific neighbors. The first one that comes to mind is Sue, who showed up on my doorstep when we moved to Holland, Michigan. She arrived with chicken soup, cupcakes, and some magazines for me to read. She had heard my husband was traveling in his line of work and figured out that with three kids aged six and under, I could use some help. What a perceptive woman. As I was recovering from the flu, I knew she was heaven-sent.

Donna had me over for cookies and tea the second week we were in Cleveland. A Chicago neighbor, Lanie, several weeks pregnant, took me for a quick trip to the ER one evening. And Betty, our Mooresville neighbor with the cute Southern drawl, let me use her shower when our water was shut off. I could go on and on with the great neighbors I've had who took the initiative to help me.

Looking back over the years, I see how God has provided people in my life when family wasn't available. While we run circles in our errand-mobiles, we need to slow down and meet those who live around us. Taking a few minutes to inquire about one's family or offering to pick up something at the store for them can go a long way.

New or not, as Christ's hands and feet, we should be alert to the needs of others. As His disciples, He charges us to accomplish kind acts. That's what should be on our "to do" list.

Let's make it a point to become the neighbor we've always wanted.

Day 38

Partners...

I thank my God every time I remember you. In all my prayers for all of you, I always pray with joy because of your partnership in the gospel from the first day until now, being confident of this, that he who began a good work in you will carry it on to completion until the day of Christ Jesus.

Philippians: 1:3-6 NIV

The Philippian church was the first church planted in Europe; a breakthrough for the gospel to be shared with the entire world. The apostle Paul loved this church for many reasons: the main one being that the Philippian church was a generous church. He knew he could count on the Philippians for support. With many problems in the other new churches, the Philippians encouraged him.

Generosity of money, spirit, and time is vital to grow a genuine community. I know missionaries who have donated their lives to serving Christ in a small and relatively unknown country. They have given up any claim to earning a good living or a comfortable life so they can be a light somewhere else. These believers radiate joy as they have learned to lay down their life for others.

You and I are missionaries when we pick up stakes and head out for unknown territories. And as a fellow missionary, I send you Paul's prayer: *That he who began a good work in you will carry it on to completion until the day of Christ Jesus.* I send you this prayer as you unpack your dishes, arrange your kitchen, go to your first parent-teacher conference, walk across the street to meet new neighbors, walk into a strange church for the first time, and open your house to new acquaintances who will hopefully turn into friends.

You and I are in partnership with God to follow His plan and know He will complete the good work He's begun. Underneath the packing material, banged up furniture, and sore muscles, He's got a blueprint—a life of joy for each of us.

Day 39

Blessings in real time...

I believe that I shall see the goodness of the LORD in the land of the living!

Psalm 27:13 RSV

*I*f I could say one thing about my moves, I'd say I've eventually seen the good side of a new area. Now I won't say I immediately stepped into some rosy attitude. Often I'd pout and compare the new area with the old community, but after unpacking boxes, I'd start to notice things I liked in my new community.

Cleveland surrounded itself with a greenbelt that rivaled any municipality. Zionsville, Indiana, with its brick-paved Main Street and vintage houses took me back to another era. West Michigan had some of the most serene beaches anywhere in the state and Chicago filled me with the ultimate in cuisine and big city bustle. When we moved to Greenville, South Carolina, I fell in love with the downtown area which was built around a river. People could sit on large flat rocks that lined the riverbank and use their laptops while sunning themselves at lunch. Each of these locations has a permanent niche in my heart and memory. I am richer for having experienced so many different areas of our country.

Many times when I would complain about an area, God would remind me to "seek the good of the land."

If you are struggling with living in a particular area, ask God to open your eyes to its unique beauty. He will lead you to activities, malls, and shops, and show you social opportunities where you will find community and all kinds of bonuses that you might miss without His guidance.

It may take time, but it's there.

Day 40

Homeless...

Jesus replied, "Foxes have holes and birds of the air have nests, but the Son of Man has no place to lay his head."

Matthew 8:20 NIV

Sometimes we need to get an eternal perspective on life. We may be discouraged as we struggle to fit into our new community. This verse reminds us how Jesus never seemed to fit in: "Foxes have holes and birds of the air have nests, but the Son of Man has no place to lay His head." He knew His life on earth was temporary and He longed to get back to His community called heaven.

We may not have the close-knit fellowship we had in another town. We may crave living closer to family, but now many miles separate us from those loved ones. Whatever our heart longs for, Jesus had that same longing.

Hebrews 4:15 tells us how Jesus is our High Priest and has experienced all the heartaches we will ever know on earth. He suffered a friend's betrayal, religious leaders plotting against Him, and He lacked any physical dwelling as a home. Even so, He suffered on a cross knowing He'd paved the way for many to join him in the community of heaven. When we arrive in eternity, we will look at all our earthly treasured *needs* and *desires* and see them as unimportant as a thirty-year-old cassette tape that's been pitched into the hall closet for the Goodwill, as we experience the real music praising Him.

Now that's genuine community.

Think it through...

I can't close this little book without giving my readers a chance to join the eternal community.

The Bible says in Romans 10:9 that, "If you confess with your mouth, 'Jesus is Lord,' and believe in your heart that God raised him from the dead, you will be saved."

Now, don't let that word "saved" confuse you. What it refers to is turning from all our selfishness and receiving His gift. When we do, we are saved from a life of loneliness and isolation. We are prepared to go to heaven because of Jesus's sacrifice. It's as though He says, "I've got you covered." And, by the way, there's a huge banquet being prepared for us. We will have the best community we can ever imagine.

If you haven't already asked Jesus to take control of your life, you can do so now with a simple prayer from your heart. Life flies by quickly. Consider His promise. He's waiting with outstretched arms to welcome you.

Forty Tips for Transitioning to a New Zip Code

Before the move:

Figure out what you will say to friends—especially neighbors.

1. Don't tell the kids too soon …it will be all over town.
2. Start packing up delicate items such as good china.
3. Put paper towels and cleaner under every sink for a quick clean-up before a "showing."
4. Keep an empty shelf or drawer in the kitchen or family room for hiding last- minute paper piles and other "stuff."
5. The back seat of a car is a great place for hiding laundry baskets.
6. Keep your house aired out and smelling fresh.
7. Try to keep kitchen counters clear.
8. Put up personal photos.
9. Work on packing a little every day.
10. Schedule time for dinner dates and coffee to say goodbye to friends.
11. Keep the lines of communication open with your children (especially teenagers).
12. Let your children express their anger or sadness about moving.
13. Try to take a few trips to the new location. The more the better.

14. Let your children give suggestions about what kind of house they would like.

15. Let your children know they can suggest, but you and your spouse pay the mortgage.

16. Go online and find community activities in your new town.

17. Stop doing a lot of cooking and start using paper plates to make life easier.

18. Accept offers of help for packing.

19. De-clutter even if you have to rent a storage unit.

20. Advertise your junk on Craigslist or Freecycle.

21. Do all the fun stuff you can in your old home. If you're moving to a warmer climate, make sure you take the kids sledding one last time.

22. Create the feeling of a team in your family…we're all in this together.

23. Remind yourself you will have friends in the new location.

24. Prepare a few boxes for the first days at the new home.

25. See www.ChangingZipCodes.com for list.

Your New Community

1. If you are driving a long distance, try to break up the trip and make it a mini vacation.
2. Have special treats and favorite toys for small children in the car.
3. Get beds set up and kitchen items unpacked first.
4. Don't do any major redecorating for a while...you might change your mind.
5. Hang out in the front yard and take walks to meet neighbors. Be available.
6. Search www.meetup.com for a great way to find local clubs and associations.
7. Call your friends back home and cry if you feel like it.
8. Call your friends back home and keep whining and complaining to a minimum.
9. Find a coffee shop or meeting place where locals hang out.
10. Talk to shop owners about your new town. Sometimes they're your first friends.
11. If you are a mother of small children, check for the local MOPS (Mothers of Preschoolers) online.
12. Pray for the right connections. Your Heavenly Father cares about your transition.
13. Realize it takes about three years to have a home feel like home.
14. Thank God for the opportunity to expand your horizons in a new adventure.
15. Expect God to meet you at every turn in the road.

Resources

Page 18 quote from *The Neurotics Notebook* by Mignon McLaughlin,
Published by Bobbs-Merrill, 1963.

Page 18 quote by C.S. Lewis from
http://www.quotationspage.com/quote/37800.html.

CPSIA information can be obtained at www.ICGtesting.com
Printed in the USA
LVOW062149230812

295738LV00001B/239/P

9 780984 765553